HOW I MAGICALLY UNSTUCK MY LIFE IN THIRTY CRAZY DAYS

HOW I MAGICALLY UNSTUCK MY LIFE IN THIRTY CRAZY DAYS WITH BOB PROCTOR

BOOK 3

SANDY GALLAGHER

MEDIA

Published 2025 by Gildan Media LLC
aka G&D Media
www.GandDmedia.com

Front cover design by Patti Knoles

Interior design by Meghan Day Healey of Story Horse, LLC.

Library of Congress Cataloging-in-Publication Data is avail-
able upon request

ISBN: 978-1-7225-0649-0

10   9 8 7 6 5 4 3 2 1

For Bob Proctor

You taught me to spread love everywhere I go
by spreading love everywhere you went.
You are the magic in this story of hope.

Sandy

CHAPTER ONE
LOST

Chloe stared at her laptop screen, feeling lost. She hadn't been able to concentrate on anything since her mentor, Sarah, shared her diagnosis of stage four cancer three weeks before. They'd talked some on the short plane ride back to L.A. that day, but mostly they just held each other. Some of the initial shock still lingered with Chloe, like a stubborn nightmare that refused to fade. Some mornings, she woke up thinking it had been exactly that—a nightmare. But then reality would set back in, and she was forced to try and find a way to accept the truth.

She felt like Sisyphus. Just when she thought she had accepted the situation and was finally turning her focus to what was next, she found herself at the bottom of the hill, pushing that same boulder of truth back up. It was exhausting—and that admission made her feel even worse. Now was not the time to be tired or sad or shocked. Sarah needed her. Chloe had to be ready. She just couldn't figure out how.

A text notification popped up on her phone. It was Sarah!

Hey, Chloe! Let me know when you have time for a quick video call. :)

Chloe's fingers flew. *Hey, Sarah! Now's good.*

Awesome! Sarah replied. *Give me just a minute.*

The last time Chloe had spoken to her, Sarah told her she needed a few weeks for further testing, talking with her leadership team, and deciding on next steps. Chloe shook her head. She still couldn't believe that Sarah had spent the last three days of the retreat dealing with the diagnosis. She couldn't imagine what that must have been like for her. It made sense that her mentor needed some time to wrap her head around things and figure out her options. With no choice but to wait for Sarah to reach out, Chloe did her best to busy herself with work.

And there was plenty of work to take care of. Between smaller writing projects with various news publications, the series on the nature of success for the SFGATE website, her ongoing novel series with her publisher, and her new novel based on her experience with the PG Institute's program, she had more than enough on her plate.

She spent the first week cleaning up the smaller projects while letting both current and potential clients know she was stepping away from the keyboard for at least a few weeks. She assured them that she'd reach out when she was actively writing again—though she kept to herself the distinct possibility that she was leaving journalism behind for good.

The thought scared her, but only slightly. The opportunities with the institute were far greater than practically anything she'd be able to build with a solo writing career. Besides, she found the prospect of running the institute more exciting. As alien and scary as it was to think of running a multimillion-dollar company, it just *felt* right. Chloe had spent years hoping to someday reach a point where her writing influenced the world. Now that she'd finally achieved it, she half-expected to feel a little pushback from herself at pivoting to a different field.

But she felt no such hesitation. What the institute offered was already quite close to her life-long dream. It was even a bit inaccurate to call it a pivot; it was more of a slight shift. She still had the ability to maintain and grow her independent fiction writing career; she was merely swapping the journalism work for the institute. Although the institute would likely require the vast majority of her time and energy, at least for the first few years, she'd always be able to chip away at her fiction writing on the side. As long as she didn't overpromise to her publishers, she'd be fine.

Furthermore, running the institute provided her with a unique and intriguing opportunity—writing fiction, or even her own memoir—through the lens of the institute's teachings. This was something she'd briefly discussed with Sarah before the catastrophic news. Sarah loved the idea, even suggesting that they launch their own publishing company. The thought of helping members tell their stories as a way for the institute to inspire and educate made perfect sense. The possibilities of what they could do with an entire division dedicated to the prospect got

Chloe fired up. She even had some ideas on how to go about it. She hoped Sarah would reach out soon. In addition to the more important issue of Sarah's prognosis, Chloe wanted her blessing on a few things before investigating the publishing division any further.

Weeks two and three since last hearing from Sarah were spent writing the nature of success series, conducting research for book two of her novel series, and above all, incorporating the final six lessons of the program into her life. Practicing the program was bittersweet—a cloud of fear and suspense hung over everything related to it, but Chloe forced herself to continue. Whatever was to come with Sarah's diagnosis, it wouldn't serve Chloe or anyone else to avoid the program. As she kept at it, she realized that continuing to practice its teachings was more important than ever.

Chloe focused on lessons seven, eight, and nine, which provided some surprisingly apt insights that aided her in her current situation. These were uncertain times, and viewing her fear for Sarah's future through the lens of lesson seven's Terror Barrier helped fortify her resolve. With lesson eight's message of the Power of Praxis, she was able to recommit herself to the program, helping her get back on track with the Three R's and her daily journaling—both of which focused her attention on solutions instead of problems. And the information about attitude in lesson nine helped her control her mindset, reminding her to look at each day—and even the uncertain future—from a confident, balanced perspective that kept her emotions in check and her conscious mind sharp. In some vague way she couldn't quite put her finger on, she also derived some solace from the program, as if doing so brought her closer to Sarah.

Yet even with all the practice, even with the sense of solace, she still found herself in moments like the present one—staring at her monitor, lost. She knew she'd accomplished more in the past few weeks than it felt. She knew she was taking a proactive approach to the problems before her, leveraging the program to ensure that the outside world didn't dictate her thoughts, emotions, and behaviors. In short, she knew she was doing everything right—but sometimes, it just didn't feel that way. She sighed, shaking herself free of the daze she was in. Perhaps that slight feeling of uncertainty was a good thing. It meant she wasn't wallowing in familiar misery but was instead pushing ahead despite the questions, despite the unknown.

Chloe's video app appeared on her laptop screen, a happy ringtone alerting her to an incoming call. She clicked on the prompt, the call connected, and Sarah appeared. Chloe did her best to hide her reaction. Sarah looked—different. She still looked healthy, but something was off. Her features were slimmer, withdrawn. Her skin lacked its typical glow, and her brown hair appeared dull, pulled back in a quick ponytail. Thankfully, her dark brown eyes were vibrant and happy, if a little tired.

"Hey, you!" Sarah said, beaming. "How've you been?"

"Hey, Sarah!" Chloe answered, matching her smile. "Been good. How about you?"

"Oh, it's been a roller coaster."

"I bet. How are you feeling? Any news?"

"Yeah, some good, some bad. All in all, I'm feeling good. Sorry for the delay. I thought I'd get back to you by now, but there's been a lot going on."

Chloe waved a hand. "No worries at all. I'm just glad you're feeling OK."

"I am, thanks." Sarah opened her mouth, then closed it, appearing hesitant. She cleared her throat and started again. "The thing is, there might not be a great deal of time, so—"

"What?" Chloe said, unable to help herself. "Why?"

"There *might* not be, that's the key word. But that doesn't mean we should waste it. Now that I'm armed with some information and have talked with my leadership team, I'm ready to turn my attention to the most important piece of the puzzle—you."

"OK," Chloe said. "Whatever you need."

"How's your work? Are you caught up?"

Chloe nodded. "Almost completely, yeah. I've finished all my contributing pieces, and most recently, the nature of success series. I just need to have a talk with Frank about that. Book two of my novel series is ahead of schedule, so I have plenty of time for that. I'm basically free."

"Good." Sarah hesitated again. "Are you still interested in my offer? Taking over the institute?"

"I was hoping you were going to take it off the table. But yes, I'm willing."

"That's great news. Before we even think about making it official, I want to make sure you're comfortable with everything the role entails. I think you already know that it's a tremendous undertaking. I don't say that because I think you need reminding, but to ensure that you're going into this with open eyes. Taking this on will undoubtedly change the course of your life. This may sound great, but I mean that in every sense of the phrase. I'm concerned that it may keep you from a life trajectory that you prefer, that it'll keep you from experiencing things you want for yourself. You know what I mean?"

"I do, yeah," Chloe said. "I've been thinking about the same thing, and as best as I can tell, I'm still up for it. There's a ton of overlap between this and what I've already envisioned for myself. So don't think for a second that you're keeping me from anything. My eyes are open."

Sarah leaned back, a relieved smile on her face. "Oh, that's so good to hear. Thank you, Chloe."

"No, thank *you*. So tell me what you need."

"Right. I thought you could come see me at home." She gestured toward the bay window behind her, overlooking green fields and a distant tree line. "I have a ranch outside Lexington, Kentucky. It's a great place to get away and gain some perspective. We can talk about the institute, what your future would look like, and see if it's something you still want to commit to. If so, then we'll go about prepping you for the role."

"Sounds great," Chloe said. "I'll pack a bag and be on the next flight out."

"Let me send the jet," Sarah said. "I'll text you the details. It should be there around midday tomorrow."

"I won't argue with that."

"And Chloe," Sarah said, her smile genuine, "I want you to know that whatever you decide about the institute, all that stuff is secondary. I really just want to see my friend again."

Tears welled in Chloe's eyes. "That's all I want too."

"I'll see you soon."

"OK."

As soon as Sarah ended the call, Chloe took a long, shaky breath. Sarah clearly knew more than she was letting on, but Chloe couldn't blame her for not sharing it just yet. Sarah would tell her when she was ready, and that meant face-to-face. Sadly, there was no way around the fact that whatever Sarah knew, it wasn't good.

Once again, Chloe stared at her laptop screen, feeling lost.

CHAPTER TWO
The Ranch

The flight to Lexington in Sarah's private jet took a little under five hours. Chloe spent that time tweaking the final draft of her series for Frank, the editor who had started her on her journey by having her cover a seminar of Sarah's for L.A. Local News. Inspired by Chloe's example, Frank had moved on to SFGATE, a news website for the San Francisco Bay Area, and commissioned Chloe to write a multipart series on the nature of success.

Attaching her draft in an email, Chloe told Frank she'd let him know soon when they could chat about it, alluding to some personal stuff she had to take care of first. Not for the first time, she pondered the idea of flying out to visit him. If she ended up getting the green light from Sarah on a few things, she was going to need him.

The fasten-seatbelt light dinged as Jane, the pilot, came over the intercom. "Miss Daniels, we're beginning our approach. We'll be touching down in sunny Lexington shortly."

Fifteen minutes later, the engines thrummed as the jet taxied along the runway, coming to a stop outside the first of a row of hangars on the edge of the airfield. A sleek black Mercedes with tinted windows sat nearby, a man in casual business attire standing next to it.

Charlie, the copilot, appeared from the cockpit, moving to the back to retrieve Chloe's luggage. "Is there anything I can do for you before you depart, Chloe?"

"Nothing at all, Charlie, thank you," Chloe replied, packing her laptop in her messenger bag.

Jane opened the passenger door and lowered the staircase. "All set, Chloe. Miss Garner has us on standby in case you're needed elsewhere. We're only a phone call away."

"Thank you, Captain." Chloe slung her bag over a shoulder and made her way up the aisle. "The more we fly together, the more I find myself looking for any reason to be elsewhere."

Jane laughed. "Elsewhere is the best destination in the world."

As Chloe approached the car, the man reached for her luggage. "Good afternoon, Miss Daniels. I'm Jack, an assistant of Sarah's. I'll be taking you to the ranch."

"Nice to meet you, Jack. Call me Chloe, please."

"Chloe it is," Jack said. "One moment and I'll get your door." After placing the luggage in the trunk, he opened the door to the back seat, gesturing Chloe inside as he gave her a slight bow.

Settled in the driver's seat, Jack smiled from the rearview mirror. "It's about thirty minutes to the ranch, if traffic is decent. You ready?"

"Let's do it!" Chloe said.

Taking a highway east out of Lexington, the countryside soon changed to winding back roads and rolling green hills, interspersed with small towns and hamlets surrounded by farmland and horse ranches. Corral fencing ran for miles, denoting pastures and property lines as it crisscrossed the landscape.

Jack turned onto a random road surrounded by trees, slowing to navigate its many twists and turns, and eventually coming to a stop before a large wrought-iron gate. He passed a keycard over the scanner at a small security kiosk, the double doors of the gate swung inward, and the car rolled through.

"Whoa," Chloe breathed, lowering her window to get a better look at the grounds. The narrow, paved road branched off in different directions, intersecting expansive swaths of manicured lawns and the occasional copse of oak, ash, and white pine. They passed a large two-story horse barn, next to which sat a training ground of some sort. A few riders on tall, gleaming horses circled the edge of the large dirt rectangle as a woman stood in the center, hands on her hips, calling out instructions.

As the car topped a small rise in the road, Chloe got a glimpse of the true scale of the property. Sloping gently downhill, fields and pastures stretched on for miles, all surrounded by dense trees in the far distance. Near the top of their slightly elevated position, Jack pulled up in front of a sprawling three-story ranch-style house, white, with black shutters at the windows, its peaked roof accented by several dormers. It looked as if it had been there for generations. And perhaps it had—bookended by two gigantic oak trees. Chloe noticed old windows and a lack of vinyl siding, giving the house a classic, well-maintained feel.

The white gravel of the semicircle drive crunched under the car's tires as Jack slowed to a stop. "Here we are, Chloe," he said, placing it in park before exiting the vehicle and opening her door.

Emerging from the air-conditioned car into the warm shade of the oaks, Chloe smiled as she breathed in the country air and felt the light breeze on her face. Jack retrieved her things from the trunk and placed them on the creaky stairs leading to the front porch. A moment later, the front door opened, revealing Sarah.

"Chloe!" she cried. "You made it!"

"Sarah!" Chloe closed the short distance to the porch, climbing the small set of stairs before enveloping Sarah in a hug. "You look great." The lie caused a pang of guilt to shoot through her gut. The changes to Sarah's features were even starker in real life. And there was less of Sarah for her arms to hold. Chloe's mentor was losing an alarming amount of weight.

"Bah," Sarah huffed, squeezing her tight. "I've looked better."

"How do you feel?"

Sarah sighed, smiling as she held Chloe at arm's length. "To be honest, I've felt better too.

But don't worry about that. Come in, come in! Jack, can you take her things to the big guest bedroom?"

"Yes, ma'am."

"Thanks," Sarah said as she led Chloe inside. The interior closely matched the exterior, mixing old-school architecture with touches of modernity. A short hallway opened onto a large sitting room on one side and a long dining room on the other before giving way to a wide, two-story foyer with a staircase leading to the second floor. Two doors on the ground floor sat on either side of the stairs, leading deeper into the house. Wainscoting and ornate hardwood trim accented every angle, and what appeared to be restored antique furniture throughout, giving the decor a luxurious yet lived-in feel. Paintings of horses and landscapes adorned the walls, which were either painted in soft tones or outfitted with patterned wallpaper, depending on the room.

"Sarah, your home is lovely," Chloe breathed.

"Thanks," Sarah replied. "My grandparents bought it many years ago. When it was passed down to me, I made a few changes and additions. I also lucked out with the surrounding land, snatching it up when a few of my neighbors put their properties up for sale. It's a far cry from the modest home my grandparents started out with, but I think they'd be proud of it."

"And the horses!" Chloe said. "You said you rode, but I had no idea they were this big a part of your life."

"Ask her about the trophies," Jack said as he shuffled past them with the luggage.

"Oh, shush," Sarah said, shooing him upstairs with a hand.

"Trophies?" Chloe echoed.

"Never mind that," Sarah replied, putting an arm around her shoulders and leading her through the door to the left of the stairs. "Let's get some tea."

After a few turns in the hallway, they entered a spacious modern kitchen next to an open dining area with floor-to-ceiling windows. The view showcased large shade trees and expansive greenery, with at least one or two more horse barns nestled in the distance.

"Is that water?" Chloe asked, peering at a sparkling line partially hidden by the hilly landscape.

"It is. A creek cuts through the southern portion of the property, about five or six miles' worth. Some call it a river, it's so big, but it was named

Allen's Creek way back when. One of the founders of the region, I think. Great fishing. And it's perfect for just getting away to think." Sarah paused as she flipped the switch on an electric kettle. "I've been spending a lot of time down there lately."

"I bet." Chloe nodded, wishing she had something better to say.

The kettle was boiling in no time, and Sarah poured water into two ornate teacups resting on saucers. "Let's have a seat," she said, grabbing the saucers and moving to the small dining table in front of the windows. As Chloe sat, Sarah set the cups down and retrieved a small serving tray from the nearby kitchen island. A selection of tea bags, honey, and other accessories accompanied a variety of cookies and crackers.

"So," Sarah started, choosing a packet of chamomile and tearing it open. "I'm sorry for leaving you with such a cliffhanger on our call, but I wanted to talk to you in person about all this."

Chloe chose what looked to be the strongest caffeinated tea. "I totally get it. Don't worry about that. Some things are best shared in person."

"Exactly." Sarah bobbed her tea bag up and down in the steaming water. "But first, a bit of business. You mentioned publishing. Putting out memoirs or fiction based on members' experiences. Is that still something you want to do?"

"It is. I've given it some more thought, and for our high-profile clients, it could provide as much marketing for them as it would for us. Kind of a win-win, you know?"

"I agree," Sarah said, squinting as she sipped her tea. "We could reach all kinds of different audiences. Speaking of different audiences, I've been toying with an idea for the past few years. I've never had time to formulate anything concrete, but I'd love to be able to speak to younger generations about this stuff. Leadership, self-improvement, self-reliance—it all begins at an early age, and curriculums are sorely lacking in this area. Getting kids to start focusing on this kind of thing early could have a tremendous impact on future generations." Sarah noticed the sly smile forming on Chloe's lips. "What is it?"

"I think I have just the person to help us with that," Chloe said. "I'll take it a step further. I bet we have a ton of corporate sponsorship potential, right?"

"Of course."

"We could expand on books, materials, and speaking tours of the school circuit with full-blown extracurricular programs for elementary and high-school students. Field trips to college campuses, where they can attend lectures, symposiums, tours. We could even establish summer camps—any number of activities dedicated to showing them the wider world, their limitless future, and how the program's principles can help them achieve their dreams."

"Chloe, I love that you think as big as I do!" Sarah laughed, raising her teacup.

Chloe joined in as they toasted. "There are two people in particular I want to talk to about it. But I think I should see them in person. It might take a little convincing."

"Where are they located?"

"The Bay Area."

"No problem," Sarah said. "I'll have Joyce notify Jane. You can go tomorrow."

"You sure?"

"Of course. You'll be back in a day or so. Then we can get some work done. You're welcome here for as long as you like. I'm hoping you can hang out for a few weeks at least—unless work calls you away."

Chloe shook her head. "I'm free as a bird. I've wrapped up everything but the novel series with my publisher, but they won't need anything from me for quite a while. I'm all yours for as long as you need me."

"Good to hear," Sarah said, growing solemn. "Sadly, I'll need you for a lot longer than I've got. But we'll just have to make do."

Chloe nearly choked on her tea. "What? What do you mean?"

Sarah met her gaze. "There's no easy way to say it, Chloe. I'm dying."

CHAPTER THREE
PLANS

"No," Chloe said. "No, there must be something they can do. Surgery, chemo . . ." Her words died as she saw the conviction in Sarah's eyes.

Her mentor reached for her hand, loosening Chloe's fingers from her crumpled packet of tea. "There's a very great deal they can do, Chloe. But ultimately, none of it improves my odds. I've had appointments with some of the best specialists from all over the country, and the consensus is that even the most generous prognosis indicates that I have six months to a year. And that time would be spent in a hospital bed, sick and barely able to move." She squeezed Chloe's hand. "That end doesn't interest me."

Chloe felt hot tears on her cheeks. "But there's no telling how it might go," she said, wiping her cheek with a sleeve. "Maybe with the right combination of treatments, you'd rally. It happens all the time. Doctors say a patient has a year to live, and they end up living ten more. Or even twenty! You can't rule out the possibilities. There's just no telling, not unless you try."

Removing Chloe's tea bag from its wrapper, Sarah dropped it in her cup. "Typically, I'd agree with you. And so would my doctors. But they've shown me the X-rays, the CAT scans. I've read the case studies and statistics. There have been many cases like mine, Chloe. The patient was going about their life, receiving regular checkups and mammograms. Then, out of nowhere, in the short months between appointments, something goes wrong—terribly wrong. 'Aggressive' doesn't begin to describe it. A more accurate term is needed. Something like 'catastrophic.'"

Chloe wept openly now. She couldn't help it. It felt as if Sarah had given up before she'd even begun. Yet deep down, she knew that wasn't quite right. Sarah wasn't so flippant in her decisions— she did her homework. She'd obviously spent the past weeks weighing everything heavily. Every option, every specialist's opinion, every word of counsel from those closest to her, all carefully considered before coming to her decision.

Yet Sarah's certainty still bothered Chloe. She'd only just learned of Sarah's predicament, and her mentor had already made up her mind. There was a hopelessness in that. It felt as though a brick wall stood before them, reaching from horizon to horizon and a mile high. On the other side of it, stretching on to forever, stood a long, happy future for them both—as business partners, but most importantly, as the closest of friends. Yet there was no way through, around, or over the wall. That future on the other side was dying, withering away as surely as the woman sitting across the table from her. It left her with a helplessness she'd never known.

"All I have left to do," Sarah continued, taking Chloe's hands in hers once again, "is decide where to focus my remaining energy. That focus will be on the PG Institute, the people and animals closest to me, and most importantly, you."

Chloe shook her head as a wave of denial washed over her. "But why, Sarah? Why me? You must have dozens of people you could entrust with the institute. People who've spent their lives studying business and relationships and personal growth. I'm new to all of it. I admit I have a knack for it, but I don't want you spending precious time teaching me everything that so many others already know. Conserve that energy, direct it toward something more worthwhile—something that makes more sense."

Sarah smiled. "What do you know about monarch butterflies?"

Chloe's bewilderment must have shown on her face, as Sarah burst into laughter. Surprising herself, Chloe joined in. "Butterflies? What the hell are you talking about?"

"Well," Sarah said, getting that twinkle in her eye when she was about to share something special. "A certain subspecies of monarch butterfly migrates from Canada to Mexico every fall, then back to Canada every spring." She spread her arms wide above her head. "Hundreds of thousands of them, in giant clouds so thick, you can barely see through them. I saw them with my own eyes once, while on a trip through Mexico. We happened upon them one morning while hiking. The sun was just breaking through the trees, its warmth causing them to wake. Every tree in the area was caked in sleeping butterflies, giving the trunks and branches a strange texture that made us wonder what we were looking at. Then, as the sun's rays hit them, they started pumping their wings, and we realized what we were witnessing.

"The forest shimmered with movement as more and more of them woke and stretched. After a few minutes, they began dropping from their perches like leaves, then catching the air with their wings and fluttering about. First just here and there, and before long, an avalanche of them—so many, you could *hear* them as they flew about, their numbers dimming the sun itself. Soon they rose higher and higher, up toward the treetops, and began heading in a southerly direction. I'd never seen anything like it.

"Of course, I had to look it up to learn more, and what I learned is as sad as it is beautiful. As you can imagine, the mortality rate for such delicate creatures on such a long journey is remarkably high. None of them survive the round trip. Those that head south from Canada and the northern U.S. do so for the first and last time. Do you know why they don't make it?"

"Why?"

"Because they aren't meant to. It's up to the next generation to continue the trip. In fact, it takes four generations to complete the cycle." Sarah leaned forward, her eyes fixed on Chloe. "You are the next generation, Chloe. I don't need to complete the journey. In fact, I'm not meant to. So preparing you for yours is the absolute best way to spend the time and energy I have left." She raised a finger, staving off another argument from Chloe. "And to answer your point, yes, I know several who would do very well running the institute, but they don't have your vision—a vision that closely resembles my own. And they don't have your voice. A voice that surpasses my own.

"I have more lessons I want to share. I always thought I'd have time to get them down properly, to refine and perfect them, making sure they stood up as a proper endcap to the existing Unstuck program. As it turns out, I don't have that time. But you do. You're the only one who can help me capture what needs to be said—to carry it with you when I'm gone and turn it into something that resonates with people, that speaks to their hearts. There isn't an MBA program in the world that

"Yeah, it feels like a different world, doesn't it? Away from the rush and hustle of everyday life. It's like the water washes all that away, leaving just the thoughts and feelings we shove aside for another time. You're allowed to be yourself, here. *Forced* to be yourself, even. Everyone should have a place like this."

"Is this where you've been working on those ideas you mentioned?" Chloe said.

"Yeah, for the most part. They've slowly been coming into focus these past few weeks."

They came upon a clearing of flat rock situated several feet above the water. A makeshift camp had been erected: old, dried logs for sitting encompassed a ring of large rocks for a firepit. The ash of innumerable past fires blackened the pale limestone outcropping in and around the pit. Sarah sat on one of the logs, facing the water, and Chloe joined her.

"I think two more lessons would do," Sarah began. "Though *lessons* may be too strong a word. Perhaps they should be a few essays to bookend the program, some final parting wisdom for members to carry with them. Whatever the case, the first one is about gratitude, I think. I find myself looking back on things, and I'm often

overwhelmed by the amount of gratitude I feel—
mostly for those I've met, those who have helped
me, and those I've been fortunate enough to help.
I think a small series of exercises on gratitude will
help members focus on what they have and how
things have changed for them as they've worked
through the program. But it's meant to include
their time before the program as well. No matter how thoroughly we allowed our paradigms
and the outside world to dictate our lives before
entering the program, we all have at least a few
reasons to be grateful—people and developments
that have changed us for the better. And these
people, these developments, are worth remem-
bering."

Chloe watched the sun sparkle off the water
as it flowed by. "That certainly sounds worth adding. And the second?"

"The second part is about loss: how remem-
brance, that focus on gratitude, can also help
prepare us for the future. The future is full of
farewells, Chloe. It's OK to mourn them, but that
mourning mustn't be allowed to rule us. Good-
byes have as much to teach us as hellos. I want
our audience to understand that loss should be
embraced. Then, equally importantly, it should

be let go. This will ensure that you approach each new day with the gratitude it deserves."

Chloe sighed. "That can be a tall order for some. How does one learn from loss?"

Sarah smiled. "By focusing less on mourning and more on celebration."

CHAPTER FOUR

FRANK AND CLAIRE

The following afternoon, after a flight to Oakland Airport and a long Uber ride, Chloe stood on the front steps of a modest house in the small town of Lafayette northeast of the city. Located on a quiet street in a green neighborhood, it was the perfect home for a couple like Frank and his wife, Claire.

Reaching for the doorbell, Chloe took a breath as she reflected on her conversation with Sarah. Chloe had shared her thoughts on the publishing division of the institute and how to go about it, as well as ideas on how to expand their audience—namely, by bringing aspects of the program to students of all ages. Sarah had especially liked that last prospect and how they could use publications to make it happen. Chloe received Sarah's blessing on all fronts, and her mentor suggested that she start right away on a memoir of her experience with the program—which would be used as the subject of her first speaking tour on behalf of the institute. Chloe found it all very exciting, but to do it properly, she was going to need some help. She was going to need Frank.

The moment the doorbell rang, an uproar of high-pitched barking sounded from deep inside the house, growing louder every second. Moments later, a soft thud hit the inside of the door, accompanied by more barking. Chloe heard Claire's muffled voice on the other side.

"Duke, stop! Take a breath before you pass out, would you please? Frank, can you—let go of my shoe! Hey!"

Chloe hid a smile as the door opened a crack.

"Chloe!" Claire kept glancing down behind the door. "Ow! Frank! One second, Chloe."

"Come here, you!" Chloe heard Frank call out.

"Careful," Claire said. "He's still a puppy."

"Puppy, my foot," Frank said. "Hey, settle down! OK, I got him."

Claire swung the door open and stepped aside. "Sorry," she said over Duke's excited barking. "He runs outside, given half a chance. Come in!"

"It's so good to see you two!" Chloe said, slipping in so Claire could close the door. "This place is lovely."

"Thanks, it's just a rental," Frank said, struggling with Duke, who was doing everything possible to escape his grasp. "Can you pet this little devil? He'll calm down a bit once he gets to know you."

"Aw, come here, Duke," Chloe said, taking him from Frank. She laughed as the little Morkie immediately began licking her face and sniffing her hair, his barking turning to excited whining.

"Careful, he might pee on you," Frank said.

"I set up some tea and snacks in the dining room," Claire said. "Don't bother to take your shoes off. Come on through."

Chloe followed them down the short hallway to an open kitchen and adjoining dining area. A large hardwood table sat next to a row of windows overlooking the side yard. A number of boxes lay strewn about the place, against the walls and stacked in corners. "How's the move-in going? You guys look almost done."

Claire gestured her to a seat as she picked up the teapot from the serving tray in the middle of the table. "Oh, it went well enough. We haven't moved in ages, so it was a bit of a trial. Just a few more boxes, mostly Frank's things." She arched an eyebrow at him.

"I know, I know. I'm working on it. It'd help if Duke didn't mark his territory on my stuff." He held three fingers up to Chloe. "Three times, this little mongrel has peed on my boxes. He's got it out for me, I tell you."

"Oh, nonsense," Claire replied with a sniff.

"Yeah?" Frank retorted. "Then tell me, how many times has he peed on your things, hm?"

Claire's eyes went wide and innocent. "Why, now that you mention it—none."

"Exactly," Frank huffed.

"He is a handful, isn't he?" Chloe said. Duke bounced around her lap, licking her face and nibbling the collar of her blouse and trying to climb onto the table—a little bundle of energy she could barely contain.

"That's one way of putting it," Frank growled.

"But he's learning," Claire insisted. "We taught him to sit and shake. Though house-training is proving a bit of a challenge."

Frank dunked his tea bag up and down, glaring at the dog. "Yeah, well, enough about that one.

You said you had some big news, Chloe. What's up?"

"First, how's everything on your end?" Chloe asked. "The job, the program, all that stuff."

"Going real good," Frank said, nodding. "Job is great. They love your series, by the way. They're likely going to put out a new installment every month. That'll get them six months down the road, but I'm sure they'd love to have you write something else, if you have a mind to. The program's going really well too. Things started clicking into place after we talked, and knowing that there are six more lessons helps me keep things in perspective. It's clear that this is a marathon, not a sprint, so I don't have to have everything perfect."

"Exactly," Chloe said. "This isn't a final draft you're taking your red pen to before throwing it back on the reporter's desk."

Frank chuckled through a mouthful of sugar cookie. "Claire, of course, is already diving into the last six lessons."

"But that's partly because I'm not working at the moment," Claire said. "With the move-in and the puppy, I'm taking some time before making any decisions on that front. So I've had more time to focus on the program."

"School administration, right?" Chloe asked.

"That's right," Claire said. "There are some great school districts in the area. I need to start polishing my résumé."

"There may be no need," Chloe said, petting Duke where he lay on her lap, tuckered out for the moment.

The couple raised their eyebrows in unison. "Oh, really?" Claire said. "That piques my interest."

"Sure does," Frank said. "What's up, Chloe?"

"Well," Chloe began, "there are some exciting things in the works, but in order to share it, I have to get the bad news out of the way first." She ran her fingers through the fine hair of Duke's coat. "There's no way to say it except to say it, so . . . Sarah was recently diagnosed with cancer."

"No!" Claire said, bringing a hand to her mouth as Frank leaned back in his seat, looking grim.

"She doesn't have long," Chloe continued. "She has a few months at most. Mainly because she's turned down most of the treatments. They would just leave her in bed, too weak to do anything. She'd rather spend her remaining time looking forward, not back."

"But she's so young," Claire said, glancing at Frank. "We didn't even get a chance to meet her."

"You may yet," Chloe said. "She wants a great many things in place while she still has the strength to oversee them. That's where you two come in."

"Us?" Frank said. "What could we possibly have that she wants?"

"Your unique ability to help me," Chloe answered. "I'm taking over the institute for her."

Claire gasped. "How exciting! Of course you are. You're the perfect fit."

"Sarah seems to think so," Chloe said with a shrug. "I'm learning that it's pointless to argue with her. I've got a lot of support from her leadership team, who I'm meeting later this week. However, I have her blessing to bring onboard anyone I want. And we've got a project I think you two might be interested in."

Frank shared a surprised smile with Claire. "We're all ears."

"We're starting two major projects. The first is a few essays I'll be writing, with Sarah's guidance. They'll likely be added to the end of the program, as a bit of parting wisdom. The other, far larger project is our goal to establish a publishing division for the institute. We plan to publish memoir-style books from our members, highlighting their experiences with the program. We'll offer coaching, editing, publishing, and marketing. Not only will these books help market the institute, but they'll help our members market their own brands and companies. They'll also help our members process their experiences while inspiring readers to go on their own journeys of self-discovery and self-improvement.

"It's a pretty big undertaking, but I thought you two might be interested. I know you've just started at the Gate, Frank, but we think if the two of you were made codirectors of the division, you'd be able to stay at your current position and focus on the institute in your off time. And if you ever decide you'd like to leave the Gate and make this a full-time thing, that door would always be open.

"Claire, your administrative skills would allow everything to be managed properly. Maybe even more importantly, your time spent with students of all ages will come in handy for another aspect of the division—we'd like to focus on content for younger audiences. Everyone from elementary school through college kids. With Frank's editing skills and your knowledge of school curricula and how to speak to young people, I think you two would make the perfect team. And we'd like to give some serious thought to expanding what we can do for younger audiences—an extracurricular program, perhaps an entire youth organization, with field trips, summer camps, the whole nine yards. Your thoughts on all that would be invaluable, Claire. Most all of this can be done remotely, with just a few meetings at the Lexington headquarters now and then throughout the year. What do you guys think?"

"I'm in," Claire said.

Chloe laughed. "Well, that was easy. What about you, Frank?"

Frank rubbed his chin with a fingertip, his eyes on Claire. "It's an intriguing offer, but book publishing? I don't know a ton about it."

"It's hardly different from journalism," Chloe said. "You'll have a team of writing coaches and editors in place. You and Claire will take a red pen to the manuscripts, showing them how to improve their stories and speak directly to their specific audiences—just like editing news articles.

We'll have people in place to see to the nuts and bolts of the publishing process, and the marketing team will take care of the rest. You can learn all the rest on the job. And with Claire and me overseeing the entire process, you'll have all the support you need. I know it's a bit different from what you're used to—"

"But that can be a good thing," Claire finished.

She gave her husband a meaningful look as he rubbed his forehead, considering. After a few moments, he nodded.

"As Frank has said," Claire continued, "he's really enjoying his new position at the Gate. However, he's admitted to feeling a little tired of it all. The Gate is an amazing place to work; it's not that. It's the industry itself. He's been thinking about a change, and he's been thinking about it for longer than he cares to admit. Ideally, he could move toward becoming a full-time author, but that usually takes years. So maybe this is just the thing he's been looking for."

"I certainly understand the fatigue with the news," Chloe said. "Over the years, you get so used to it that you forget about that weight on your shoulders, assuming it's all just part of everyday life. And I have no doubt he could become a full-time author, but as you said, that takes time. Here's a little cherry on top: you two are invited to write your own stories, published and marketed by the institute. And as we establish more connections in the publishing industry, we'll connect Frank with those interested in publishing what he wants to write—including his new thriller series about that crack reporter."

Frank smiled. "I've barely outlined the first book yet. I'm still working on my dad's memoir."

"So you work at the institute and write in your off time," Chloe suggested. "It's perfect. How about you give it a trial run? Part-time, with the option to go full-time. Joyce is putting together some compensation packages for you both, and let me just say, they're pretty impressive."

Claire clapped her hands, causing Duke's head to shoot up from Chloe's lap. "Come on, Frank! This is exciting! Life-changing, even. You've got to take it for a test drive, at least."

"You're right," Frank said, sitting up straighter in his seat. "You're both right. I've done enough in the news business. It's time for something different. I'll always wonder *what if,* if I don't at least give it a try. Let's do the part-time thing for now—mostly because I don't want to leave the Gate hanging so soon after giving me a position. When the time comes, I'll work with them on finding my replacement."

"There's the man I married!" Claire shouted, smacking a hand on the table. She and Chloe started cheering.

"OK, settle down," Frank said.

Excited by all the noise, Duke hopped up on the table, his tail wagging in a blur as he jumped around and barked.

"Hey, you!" Frank shouted, snapping his fingers and waving the dog over. "Come here. You know better than that."

Duke scrambled across the table to Frank, nearly spilling his tea. In a flash, the dog snagged a cookie from his plate and darted out of reach.

"Why, you little—!" Duke leapt to the floor as Frank chased after him, leaving Chloe and Claire in stitches.

CHAPTER FIVE

JOYCE

The three spent the remainder of the day talking things over, eventually ordering takeout and eating dinner on the back deck. They convinced Chloe to stay the night in the guest room instead of grabbing a room near the airport. By afternoon the following day, she was back at the ranch in Lexington.

Sarah's assistant, Joyce, met Chloe at the door, waving her in. "Welcome back, Chloe. How'd it go?"

"Thanks," Chloe said, wheeling her suitcase behind her. "Mission accomplished. They're both on board."

"Wonderful!" Joyce said. "Sarah's out at one of the horse barns, talking with the barn manager and trainers. Word got around pretty quickly, so now she's in the process of breaking the news to the staff. She has a long list of friends and colleagues to get in touch with as well, but I'm making sure she spreads out that kind of thing. We need to keep her spirits up."

Chloe noticed some new flower arrangements in the foyer. "It looks like she's shared the news with a few already."

"She has indeed," Joyce confirmed, looking solemn. "For most, she hasn't shared the specifics, just that she's sick. So she's been getting a lot of get-well-soon wishes. Anyway, she should be back in an hour or so. She wanted me to show you to her study upstairs. With the new writing you two will be working on, she thought it'd be good for you to get a little more personal insight into her. You can learn a lot about someone by seeing where they work. And when Sarah's home, she's either on a horse or in her study."

"That's a great idea," Chloe said as they climbed the stairs. Leaving her suitcase at the start of the hallway leading to her guest bedroom, she followed Joyce down another hall and into a large room at the end. Located at a back corner of the house, the study was a mix of rich hardwoods and green houseplants, with large windows that allowed lots of sunlight from two directions. Sprawling ferns, spider plants, snake plants, philodendrons, and an abundance of other greenery crowded nearly every flat surface. A large desk sat at one end, opposite a sitting area in front of a fireplace, consisting of a plush leather sofa with end tables and a coffee table. A small bar near one of the windows contained an assortment of bottles and glasses, complete with an electric tea kettle and teacups with saucers. Fresh air from an open window mingled with the scent of old books and fireplace ash, adding to the room's cozy yet vibrant feel.

"I can see why she spends so much time here," Chloe said, setting her messenger bag in a chair.

Joyce flicked the teapot on and readied some cups. "Yeah, it's one of her favorite spots."

"How are you doing with all this?" Chloe asked, leaning against the back of the sofa. "You've been with her a long time, haven't you?"

"About five years," Joyce replied. She paused, as if considering how much to share. "It's been hard. We've had a few deep conversations since she got the news, and again when she decided not to pursue treatment. That was a hard one. I was dead set against her decision not to fight it.

But then, seeing how comfortable she was with her decision, I realized I was just being selfish. It wasn't my choice to make. The best I can do for her is the same thing I've always done—whatever she needs me to do to help her achieve her goals."

Chloe shook her head. "I can't imagine how difficult it must be for you. I've known her less than a year, and a part of me still feels in shock. Like I'm losing a lifelong friend. I suppose she has that effect on people."

"She certainly does."

"But you'll be staying on after, right?"

Joyce gestured to the selection of tea as she poured water into their cups. "As the new president of the institute, that's up to you. I know Sarah planned on recommending me, but the final decision is yours."

Chloe joined her at the bar and chose a bag of Earl Grey. "Of course I want you to stay. I'll need someone to make it look like I know what I'm doing." The two chuckled as they made their way to the sofa. "But only if it's something you want for yourself."

"It is." Joyce stared at her tea, swirling the bag in slow circles. "It'll be beyond strange to carry on without her, but the institute has become as important to me as it is to her. I would feel like I'm failing her if I moved on just because she's no longer around. Besides, her diagnosis aside, I love this work. The travel, meeting new people, the busy schedule—always a hundred things going on at once. There's so much to organize and coordinate. I feel like I'm doing something *good*, you know? Like I'm helping build something larger than myself. I've been a personal assistant to a number of high-profile people before Sarah, and they were great experiences, but they were just jobs. No one's made me feel like I belong the way she has. And I like that feeling."

"Well," Chloe said, "as long as I have anything to say about it, you'll always be welcome here. And should you ever decide to explore other options, you'll always have a spot waiting for you. That said, I'm so glad you want to stay—and more than a little relieved."

"Thank you, Chloe. That means a lot. Especially with this talk of expanding on the lessons and establishing a publishing division. Sarah's been batting around these ideas for a couple years now. It'll be exciting to finally make them a reality. Oh! That reminds me." She set her cup down and moved to the bookshelves. "You'll be getting together with Sarah soon to go over the new writing, right?"

"Yeah, I imagine we'll be working on it this week."

"Great," Joyce said, sounding distracted as she ran a finger along a line of books before rifling through stacks of papers on the desk. "There was an old notebook here somewhere, a favorite of Sarah's. Where—ah! Here it is." She made her way back to the couch, holding a small leather-bound journal. She handed it to Chloe. "This belonged to Bob Proctor. It's a collection of essays, thoughts, and musings. She showed it to me a while back. There's some really good stuff in there. I'll often find her flipping through it while she works on scripts for her speaking events, and of course around the anniversary of his passing. I've read through it a few times, and I have no doubt there are some nuggets in there she'd love to add to the new program material."

"This is perfect!" Chloe said as she skimmed through it. The polished leather appeared ancient, covered in scrapes and scratches. The cover had a tiny length of wood attached to it, smaller than her pinky, with a leather cord attached to the back cover, which could be wrapped around the small peg on the front cover to keep it closed. The pages were filled with fine cursive writing from what appeared to be a fountain pen—everything from single-line quotes to several-page essays, all with doodles and notes scattered throughout the margins.

"That's just one of them," Joyce informed her. "I'm sure she wants you to go through them. She has a few more around somewhere."

"I do indeed!" a voice called from the doorway.

"Sarah!" Chloe said.

A look of concern painted Joyce's face as she got up. "That was quick. Everything OK?"

"Of course, of course," Sarah said, waving her off. "I forgot the trainers have a three o'clock class with some girls from the local 4-H. I didn't want to keep them. Anthony gave me a ride back to the house."

"Decaf?" Joyce asked, readying some tea.

"Please," Sarah replied, heading for the sofa with a sigh.

Chloe moved to Joyce's spot and patted her old one. "You have more journals of Bob's?"

"Yeah," Sarah said, "and as usual, Joyce is right on the money. I'd love for you to go through them all. They've been a huge influence on me over the years, and I think there are a few themes and subjects we could extrapolate on to give the program the final touches we're looking for."

"Exciting stuff," Chloe said, rubbing her fingertips over the pliable cover. "I'll go through them and come up with a short list of things we might want to use."

"Actually," Joyce said, bringing Sarah her tea before leaning against the arm of the sofa, "there might be more in the attic. We had some major renovations done a few years ago, not long after Bob passed. We shuffled so much stuff around before finally deciding to store it until the construction was complete."

Sarah gasped. "You're right. But then that corporate speaking tour was moved up, and we took off before the renovations were done. We were on the road for about a month, and by the time we came back, it was all we could do to get the furnishings back in place before having follow-up meetings and setting up the program teams for all the new clients. That was a busy time."

"I'll poke around up there and see what I can find," Joyce said.

"I bet that's where my notes for the *Unstuck* book wound up, remember?" Sarah said.

"Ugh, we looked everywhere for those," Joyce laughed. "Good thing we had them saved in the cloud."

"I'm all for the digital age," Sarah said, "but there's just something about having a hard copy in front of you. Feels more real than a computer screen. Anyway, how are Frank and Claire? Are they interested?"

"More than interested," Chloe said. "They're both ready and willing. Frank will be part-time until he gets his feet wet. Claire and I are sure he'll love it, so it's only a matter of time before he helps find and train his replacement at the Gate."

"Excellent news," Sarah said, sighing again. "Well, you have the run of the place." She gave Chloe's knee a pat as she stood. "I'm going to grab a few winks before dinner. Joyce can help with anything you need."

"Sounds good," Chloe said, doing her best to hide her concern.

"I'll set dinner for five or so?" Joyce asked.

"That would be lovely," Sarah replied, taking her tea with her. She paused at the doorway. "It's so nice having you here, Chloe. Whatever you need, just let us know."

"I will, thanks Sarah," Chloe said. "I'm really glad to be here."

After Sarah disappeared around the corner, the two shared a look.

"Is she OK?" Chloe whispered.

"Yeah," Joyce said, nodding her head. "She's been lying down more often lately. Probably the best thing for her."

"Yeah," Chloe echoed. She paused, unsure if she should ask. "Is there really a training session with 4-H at three o'clock?"

Joyce hesitated, her eyes lingering on the doorway. "No . . . no, there isn't."

CHAPTER SIX
PROGRESS

The attic was more a large apartment than a dusty storage space. Though much of it was dedicated to old furnishings, boxes, and other items beneath sheets of plastic, the space boasted a kitchenette, a small bath, and plenty of light from the house's many dormers. Chloe and Joyce uncovered a mahogany desk and a few chairs and tables for the living room–dining room area, and they had a queen bed moved into the bedroom so Chloe could have everything she needed in one place. With a little help from the housekeeping staff, they had everything arranged and sparkling clean within a day.

The two then went about discovering the contents of the many boxes they'd gathered in the main room. Stacks of books soon grew around them, some with notes scribbled in the margins, both in Bob's hand and Sarah's. A variety of notebooks was also discovered, most belonging to Bob, with the remainder belonging to Sarah. Regardless of the owner, many of them dated back several years, with a handful even reaching a decade or two. Having received Sarah's blessing to go through it all, they hunkered down for a few days, diving into everything. Joyce often broke away to tend to any number of things, sometimes leaving Chloe alone for hours at a time to scribble her own notes. She got lost in the books, almost all of which had clearly been reread many times by either or both of the institute's namesakes, and she reveled in the journals and diaries, gleaning fascinating insights on Sarah and her mentor, the inimitable Bob Proctor.

Sarah spent the majority of her days on the phone or running video meetings from her computer, conducting business as best she could without revealing the plans in place for the institute's immediate future. Only her team and a few trusted partners knew that the institute would soon be under new leadership—nearly all of its clients, staff, and adjacent vendors and service providers were kept on a need-to-know basis. For Joyce's part, she had a tricky time of it, canceling Sarah's upcoming speaking tour, interviews, book signings, and a host of other obligations.

Every evening, the three of them got together for dinner. Even though Sarah seemed to eat less and less at every meal, she still talked excitedly about their work. Chloe would share fascinating passages from one of Bob's notebooks, and Sarah would come alive with new ideas and interesting takes on how they could be used. Chloe began bringing a notebook with her to ensure she got everything down, incorporating them into her writing later.

The three of them carried on this way for weeks. Chloe loved the routine of it all, even going out for a jog every morning to clear her head and plan her writing. The green hills and clean country air were really growing on her. She met the barn manager, Lewis, who was always up bright and early to tend to the horses, and she promised him she'd take a few riding lessons sometime. It had been years since she'd been on horseback.

After dinner every night, the three friends lounged on the back deck, watching the sunset over a glass of wine, laughing and sharing stories about everything from school and work to men and relationships. Sometimes things were so good that Chloe forgot the sadness looming over them. She felt as if they were in an alternate dimension, where the world had stopped and they'd been given a chance to explore, share, and grow together. She learned so much about herself, the nature of life, and the potential for humankind, leading her to realize years later that her short time there had been a pivotal moment for her. One evening, as she paused to watch Sarah and Joyce gaze at the glowing horizon during a lull in the conversation, Chloe had a feeling that what she was experiencing was special. Only much later did she realize that it was one of the most memorable times of her life.

On a Thursday evening following that realization, as Chloe typed away on her laptop, she heard the telltale footsteps of Joyce making her way up the stairs. Rereading her last paragraph, she absently moved a stack of papers off the chair next to her, placing them on the small table, just out of reach of a cold cup of coffee.

"Hey, how's it going?" Chloe asked, hammering away at the backspace key. She looked up to find a haunted expression on Joyce's face. "What's wrong? What is it?"

Joyce plopped into the seat beside her, tucking an errant lock of red hair behind her ear. "Just more of the same." She shook her head. "She's getting worse. Her doctor agreed to see her at home, and he just left. He had some more test results from her latest appointment the other day." She took a deep, shaky breath. "It's bad, Chloe."

"It's OK," Chloe said, grasping her hand. "What did they find?"

"It's everywhere now," Joyce said, a tear streaming down her face. "In her lymph nodes, her brain. Her lungs are clear for now, but it's in her *bones*." Her breath hitched as she continued. "I have to confess—she made me promise to keep the worst from you this past week. But I can't anymore. She hardly eats. She gets terrible headaches and dizziness. She's even trying to hide the worst from me now. She's in a lot more pain than she's letting on." She began breaking down, her tears flowing freely. "I'm sorry I didn't tell you."

"No," Chloe said, pulling Joyce's head into the crook of her neck. Tears of her own escaped as she stroked Joyce's hair. "You didn't do anything wrong. It's OK." Joyce shook with sobs as Chloe continued to soothe her: "You're doing everything right. Don't worry about that. You've been there for her every step of the way." She pulled Joyce away and held her face in both hands, wiping her tears with her thumbs. "Do you know how lucky she is to have you? We should all be so lucky to have someone like you in our lives. I know I am. Together, we're going to make sure she has everything she needs. Everything she wants. Right?"

Joyce nodded her head. "Right." She grasped Chloe's hands and pulled them down to where their knees touched, giving them a squeeze. Sitting up, she looked to the ceiling and let out a deep breath. "Whew! I don't know where that came from. Probably been building up for a while."

"Same here," Chloe said, wiping her cheeks on her shoulders. "A good cry is a pressure-release valve. You gotta let it out." She gave Joyce's hands a final squeeze before standing up. "Then you gotta have some tea. Or something stronger. Where's that dusty bottle of bourbon we found?"

Joyce made a face. "I put it in the kitchen. But it must be bad by now, right?"

"Oh, probably," Chloe said, moving down the short hallway.

"Check the cupboard by the fridge," Joyce called.

"Got it," Chloe called back, soon returning with the bottle and two tumblers. She moved her laptop out of the way and piled some papers on top of it, making room on the table. Taking a seat, she held the bottle up to the light. "I dunno, looks kind of murky."

"Only one way to find out."

"That's the spirit!" Chloe poured a few fingers in each glass. Handing one to Joyce, she raised hers in a toast. "To being there."

Joyce smiled. "To being there."

After clinking glasses, they each took a tentative sip.

"Yeah, that's not good at all," Chloe said, smacking her lips.

"Mm," Joyce said, her expression sour. "It's terrible."

They laughed, clinking their glasses again and taking another sip.

"So," Joyce sighed, "the doctor was able to convince her to have a nurse on site. I'm going to set her up in your old room. She'll monitor Sarah's progress and help manage her pain."

"That's good," Chloe said. "The nurse can help her in ways we can't—and in ways she wouldn't want us to, no matter how much we begged her to let us."

"True. She wants to see us in a little bit. I have a feeling she wants to move the timetable up for the company meeting. It was supposed to be next week, but . . ."

"Did the doctor not give her that long?"

Joyce drained her glass. "He wouldn't say. When I walked him out and asked him, he just shrugged. A week, three months, there's just no telling. But he said he'd be surprised if it was more than a few weeks. Whatever the case, I think Sarah understands. I know she wants to spend more time with us and the horses. But she won't rest until this meeting is taken care of."

"Who are we meeting?"

"A few key members of the team. They oversee various aspects of the institute. The head of marketing, Dennis Frasier. He's a great guy. Runs the website, coordinates the livestreams, videography, helps with recruitment, tons of stuff. Linda Turner, she's the head of outreach. Runs our affiliate and coaching programs, works with nonprofits and other organizations. She'll be a big help with the youth program. I think she and Claire will get along great. Then there's Antoine Moreau, he's in charge of operations. He's like Sarah's right hand, taking care of whatever she needs done, especially when she's away on tour for extended periods. Throw in Frank and Claire as the new heads of publishing, and there you have it. With you at the tippy-top, naturally.

"We've had a few video calls with Dennis, Linda, and Antoine over the past few weeks. They're saddened, of course, but they've read your stuff and have gotten an earful from Sarah about you. They're really excited to have you at the helm."

"Really?" Chloe asked. "I figured one of them would want the spot for themselves. At the very least, I thought they'd find her decision confusing."

"Not at all." Joyce shook her head firmly. "These folks knew Bob Proctor back in the day. They all met through him, in fact. Together, they all helped the institute become what it is today. To call them loyal would be an understatement. Bob meant the world to them, as does Sarah. They trust her completely. This isn't your typical corporate leadership team, you'll see. They're going to support you the whole way, just as they have me ever since Sarah hired me. More than that, they're going to be some of your closest friends and allies. You couldn't ask for a better group of people, believe me."

Chloe arched her eyebrows. "Wow, that takes a load off my mind. Now I can't wait to meet them."

A knock sounded at the bottom of the stairs.

"That's probably the nurse," Joyce said. "Come on up!"

Footsteps sounded on the staircase, followed by a middle-aged woman in scrubs and comfortable-looking sneakers.

"Hi, Betty. This is Chloe," Joyce said. "She's a close friend of ours. She's taking over Sarah's work for her. Anything you would tell me, you can tell her."

"Understood. Nice to meet you, Chloe," Betty said.

"You too, Betty," Chloe replied. "We're really glad you're here. I'm sure Joyce has already said it, but if there's anything you need, don't hesitate to let us know."

"Thank you, I appreciate it," Betty said. "Miss Garner would like to see you both, at your convenience."

"Wonderful, we'll be right down," Joyce said.

Betty gave them a nod and a smile before heading back the way she'd come.

Chloe gathered her laptop and a notepad, throwing them in her messenger bag as Joyce wiped her face and ran a hand through her hair.

"Do I look like I've been crying?" Joyce asked.

Chloe approached her, turning her toward the light of a nearby window. "Nope," she said, brushing some lint off Joyce's shoulder and flicking a lock of hair from her collar. "How about me?"

Joyce gave Chloe the same once-over, turning her this way and that in the light. "Nope," she echoed. Reaching an arm out, she pulled Chloe into a hug. "Thanks."

Chloe hugged her back. "Thank *you*." She pulled away, meeting Joyce's eyes. "Let's go be there for her."

Joyce gave her a tight nod, and the two marched down the hallway toward the stairs.

CHAPTER SEVEN
MEMORIES AND MONARCHS

With some help from the staff, Betty had been able to convert a sitting room at the back of the house on the first floor into a bedroom for Sarah. And not a moment too soon: while Sarah prepared to meet them on the back deck, Betty took Chloe and Joyce aside and made it known that stairs were no longer an option. Sarah was growing weaker by the day.

"I convinced her to start using a cane," Betty informed them. "And I'm having some more equipment delivered in the morning, including a hospital bed and a wheelchair."

"Good to know," Joyce said. "Thank you, Betty."

A short time later, Sarah joined them on the deck. Chloe noticed that she did indeed appear weaker. She moved slower, more carefully. Though she smiled, pain sometimes flashed in her eyes, especially when she sat down. She wasn't gaunt, but she was clearly losing weight, and it showed the most in her face. Chloe wasn't used to seeing her mentor look so frail.

"Well, it looks like the jig is up," Sarah said with a sigh. "I'm sorry to keep things from you both this past week. I just can't stand the thought of you worrying about me. But seeing how quickly things are developing, it's obvious that approach doesn't serve any of us, if it ever did. In my defense, dying is new to me—so I suppose I can be forgiven for not getting it right on the first go."

The three chuckled as Joyce poured them all some tea.

"I understand your reasoning," Chloe said. "It's just hard to help if we don't know how. You've got to tell us."

Sarah took her hand and gave it a squeeze. "Thank you, my dear. I will, I promise. As long as you two promise—no more tears."

Chloe and Joyce shared a look of surprise.

"Nothing gets by our Sarah," Joyce said as the three laughed. "Fine, I promise."

"I promise too," Chloe said.

"Good!" Sarah said, squeezing a slice of lemon into her tea. "Now, as Joyce may have guessed, I'd like to move our company meeting up. We have no time to lose. Let's see if everyone can make it here tomorrow."

After a few minutes on their cell phones, the three had the meeting moved to the following day. Sarah and Joyce contacted Dennis, Linda, and Antoine, who were all currently at the company headquarters in nearby Lexington. Meanwhile, Chloe called Frank and Claire. Frank told her he'd take a personal day from work, and Chloe said she'd send the jet to fetch them in the morning. Everyone was set to meet at the house in the afternoon.

"With that out of the way," Sarah said, "what's next? Anything new and exciting?"

Chloe grabbed her laptop from her bag. "Well, I had an idea I've been working on for a while. You have all these great books upstairs and in your library, like *Think and Grow Rich* by Napoleon Hill, as well as all the writings by Bob Proctor and you. I definitely think, from our discussions, that the content you'd like to add would be best conveyed in the form of essays at the end. After reading through a ton of the stuff upstairs, it occurred to me that maybe the entire lesson plan would benefit from the same treatment—short, powerful essays from a number of different writers, one appearing at the end of each lesson."

She scooted her chair closer to Sarah and turned her laptop toward her. "I was able to match each lesson with an appropriate topic. I think it gives the reader a bit of inspiration, while providing some thought-provoking insight from a variety of influential people. Like here at the end of lesson one, we have something on the power of decisions by Bob Proctor. It goes really well with the theme of the lesson—setting and achieving your goals. Some of the essays are a mixture of passages from various writers. This one here is from an unknown author. I found it in one of Bob's journals. And the last one, for lesson twelve, is on accountability. Something you wrote in one of your journals. The rest after that is what I have so far on the new content—the last two essays, titled 'Farewell' and 'New Day.'"

"That's an incredible idea," Sarah said, her eyes bright as they devoured the words on the screen. "Breaking up the lessons with essays. Brilliant. Oh, here's one from Albert E. N. Gray.

And Thomas Troward! I remember when I first came across this."

Chloe and Joyce shared a smile as Sarah read in silence for a time.

"So many memories," Sarah mused. "I took Bob's passing hard—perhaps harder than I needed to. I received those boxes from his estate some weeks later, and I only spent a little time going through them. I always meant to get back to them and explore it all properly, but the years passed quickly. It's this kind of thing I want others to avoid with my passing. Besides, it's something I want everyone to avoid in their own lives. There's far too much mourning going on, and not nearly enough celebration."

She scrolled to the bottom of the draft and read the new essays. "I love this part you have here in the 'Farewell' essay: 'Like the Terror Barrier of lesson seven, there is a similar terror in saying goodbye. Yet this is a quite different fear, in that we have no choice but to accept it. Changing our paradigm always contains a choice—we have the option to shy away from change, to stick with the same old beliefs and habits that have kept us stuck. We have the option to succumb to our fear. But when losing a loved one, we have no such choice. We *must* face our fear. We must say our farewells, no matter how scared we are to carry on without the one we're losing.'"

"Something you mentioned the other day struck a chord," Chloe said, "and I wanted to explore it a little further. You were talking about your ex-husband and how you both agreed, years later, that your divorce was one of the best things to ever happen to your relationship. There seems to be a lot of fear in choosing to end something, even if you know it to be for the best. There's a stigma attached to endings."

Sarah smiled. "That's exactly right. Daniel and I learned that we were never happier than when we were apart."

The three laughed as Sarah leaned back in her chair, her eyes growing distant.

"But at the time, the thought of divorce seemed impossibly scary to both of us. We didn't want to say goodbye because we were both fully aligned with that stigma—endings are inherently bad. That's precisely the stigma we need to combat. In love, as in life, conclusions aren't tragedies. Like every stage preceding them, they are celebrations."

"I saw a note in your journal as well about what you and Daniel called your divorce contract," Chloe prompted.

Sarah beamed. "Yes, I remember that. Borrowing from Shakespeare, we titled it, 'Agreement to Become Better Strangers.'"

The three howled with laughter.

Sarah spread her arms wide. "But you see? We celebrated the ending of the marriage, instead of chalking it up as a loss. And we were far better for it. We remained good friends for many years until his passing. I wish I'd been able to bring that kind of celebration to Bob's life, directly after his passing. But it took several years to get there. I feel like now, with these new passages added to the program, he's finally being celebrated properly."

"As you can see, though, I have far less on the 'New Day' essay," Chloe said. "I'm still rolling it around in my head. I haven't quite picked the direction it should take."

Sarah nodded, rereading the section. "This is a good start, but I don't want to say too much on it. I think it may be best to follow your heart on this one, because ultimately it's you who needs to figure out what it means. You're the one who's going to have to live that new day after I'm gone. You're the one who's going to guide the institute through it, and all those new days to come."

"I feel like it's closely tied to the theme of celebration," Joyce remarked. "With deep mourning comes this impression that every new day is something you *have* to experience. But with celebration, every new day is something you *get* to experience."

Sarah pointed at her. "Yeah, I like that."

"I think I see what you mean," Chloe said, adjusting the laptop and typing some notes. "The two—farewells and the new day—are intertwined. And each new day is an opportunity to celebrate the farewell."

"That's good," Sarah said. "Follow that wherever it takes you."

"I will," Chloe promised, typing away.

"So, the publishing division," Sarah said. "Joyce and I both think Linda will be a big help to Frank and Claire. Is Frank sure he wants to take the plunge?"

"If it wasn't for Claire, I don't know if I'd be able to convince him to give it a go," Chloe said. "The fact that she's on board is a big motivator for him. He's a bit worried about his lack of publishing knowledge, but I can't think of a better editor. From the company-wide vision on content creation to the individual lines of the content itself, he knows exactly how to produce the most compelling ideas in the most impactful way, all while ensuring consistency across an entire body of work. I bet in another life, he'd have been an editor for a publisher. I can't think of anyone better for the job. I bet in three to six months, he'll be willing to make the transition to full-time."

"Marvelous," Sarah said. "I have a number of contacts in the industry, including the publisher of my last book."

"I'll be sure to share them with both Frank and Claire," Joyce said. "I'll schedule video calls and make introductions."

Sarah nodded. "Great, thank you. I think we'll be able to put Frank's worries at ease in short order, while giving him some amazing resources to learn more about everything. That should help him settle in and take the division in the right direction."

"That would be a big help," Chloe said. "And Claire—she's worked in two or three different school districts over the past thirty years or so. She can help steer the vision of the youth-oriented content, and she has a lot of experience working with various youth organizations. Between her network and Linda's, we're going to be able to bring our work to kids everywhere."

Sarah clapped her hands together. "So exciting! Can you feel it?"

"Sure can!" Chloe laughed. "Also, I was thinking. Given that there's no end to how big we could grow this youth-oriented work, maybe the institute could create its own youth organization."

"Ooh, that's a great idea," Joyce said.

"That's thinking big, Chloe," Sarah said. "I love it."

Chloe smiled. "I was thinking we could call it the Monarch Society."

Sarah gasped. "That is absolutely brilliant."

"She told you the butterfly story, eh?" Joyce said.

"Of course I did," Sarah said. They laughed as she raised her teacup. "To the monarchs, past, present, and future."

"To the monarchs!" Chloe and Joyce echoed.

CHAPTER EIGHT
THE MEETING

Sitting on the front porch with Sarah and Joyce, Chloe listened as the breeze moved through the two towering oak trees, bringing with it a small reprieve from the afternoon heat. She was glad Sarah had installed central air in the place some years ago: Betty had told her and Joyce to try to keep Sarah out of the heat. But the porch had plenty of shade, and they'd return inside as soon as their guests arrived.

A short time later, an SUV pulled up. The driver hopped out and held the door as Dennis, Linda, and Antoine hopped out. With a hand from Chloe and Joyce, Sarah rose to meet them as they climbed the steps of the porch. As Sarah and Joyce shared hugs with each of them, they introduced Chloe.

"It's wonderful to finally meet you," Dennis told her. A bearded man in his early fifties, Dennis had a laid-back air about him that was instantly inviting.

"Thank you," Chloe said. "It's great to meet you too."

Linda was somewhere in her late forties. Her bright smile and naturally graying hair exuded charm and authority. She extended a hand, placing the other on Chloe's shoulder. "We've heard a great deal about you, and we're all very excited to see where you lead us. I just finished your latest article on success on SFGATE. What an intriguing piece! I can't wait to read the rest."

"Thanks very much," Chloe said. "I doubt I'll be doing much writing for news outlets anytime soon, but it was a great series to end on."

"That was a collaboration with one of our other new members, if I'm not mistaken," Antoine said. Tall, lean, and easily the elder of the group, he hunched his shoulders as he shook hands with Chloe, wrapping his free hand warmly around hers.

"It was," Chloe confirmed. "Frank should be here shortly, with his wife, Claire. I think they'll be perfect for the publishing division. And there's a good chance we'll be able to woo him away from the Gate."

"Excellent," Antoine said as Sarah took his arm.

"Have you decided?" Sarah asked him.

"I have," he said. "The timing couldn't be better."

"Decided what?" Linda said, mocking suspicion.

"Why, nothing at all, my dear!" Antoine said, a look of wide-eyed innocence painting his face.

Linda leaned close to Chloe. "Always scheming, those two. You never know what they're up to."

A ripple of laughter went through the group. "You'll see soon enough," Sarah said. "What say we all head inside while we wait for Frank and Claire? We've had drinks and food laid out in the dining room."

"Good!" Dennis said, holding the front door for everyone. "Sarah said there'd be shrimp; otherwise I wouldn't have come."

"Don't worry about that. There's a platter with your name on it," Sarah assured Antoine as he helped her inside.

No sooner had the group sat around the large dining room table than Jack entered with Frank and Claire in tow. Duke struggled against Claire's arms, stealing the show as Chloe made introductions. The little Morkie shook with excitement at all the new faces, doing his best to escape Claire's grasp.

"I'm afraid to let him down!" Claire laughed.

"That's OK," Sarah told her, "go ahead. He's so cute!"

Claire set Duke down on the floor, and he immediately scrambled from one pair of legs to the next, sniffing shoes and whining in excitement. He licked every hand that came near him, his tail a blur as he basked in all the attention.

"I still don't know if it was such a good idea to bring him," Frank murmured to Chloe.

"Nonsense," Chloe said. "Sarah loves dogs. She had a Maltese once. I thought it'd be good to have him around."

As the group settled in around the table, they passed various platters of finger foods, along with pitchers of coffee and iced tea. Duke found a home in Sarah's lap, showing a great deal of interest in the goodies on the table.

"I have to admit," Sarah said, "I'm a sucker for spoiling dogs. Does he have any dietary restrictions?"

"None that we know of," Claire laughed. "Feed him whatever you like. He took the plane ride really well, so he deserves to be spoiled."

"I took the plane ride well too," Frank said. "What about me?"

"You've been spoiled enough, dear," Claire retorted.

Frank harrumphed, pointedly piling extra finger sandwiches on his plate as the gathering laughed.

"Well," Sarah said, feeding Duke a cracker, "let me thank you all for coming on such short notice. Much of the business has already been discussed in one form or another, but I thought we'd all feel better having a proper sit-down in the same room. There are some exciting things ahead for the institute, and I wanted to ensure we got things off on the right foot. The journey that Chloe in particular is about to embark upon is understandably a bit daunting for her, but I know of no better group to give her the support she needs than the leaders of the PG Institute. And with Frank and Claire coming aboard, there are exciting times ahead indeed."

Antoine raised his glass. "Hear! Hear!"

A small cheer went up as the group raised their glasses.

"With that," Sarah said, "I open up the floor to questions, comments, and ideas."

Duke barked at Sarah, eliciting laughter from the table.

"Duke from the canine division has brought a motion to the floor for more treats," Sarah announced. "Is there a second?"

"I second the motion," Linda said.

"All those in favor?" Sarah continued.

A round of "ayes" went up.

"The motion passes," Sarah stated, feeding Duke a piece of turkey as the group laughed.

"The three of us have something we'd like to share," Dennis said, glancing at Linda and Antoine.

"Please do," Sarah invited.

"We thought in celebration of the great Sarah Garner, we'd offer unlimited access to the website's courses and seminars for thirty days, culminating in a livestream celebrating your life.

We have a sizable budget set aside for promotion, but we're certain that once we share the news with various corporate partners, they'll be more than willing to chip in and help spread the word. It's not much, but we thought it'd be a great way to honor you and help spread your vision."

"Oh, that's lovely," Sarah said, placing a hand over her heart. "What a wonderful idea, thank you."

"In keeping with that," Chloe said. "I also had a thought."

"What's that, Chloe?" Sarah asked.

"Well, we've been talking so much over the past few weeks, sharing stories and ideas and everything. I was looking over some of my notes, and it's obvious that I have enough for another book. It'll take me some months to put together, and I'd like to interview the rest of the team to get more info, but I thought another Sarah Garner book at some point in the future would be a nice way to honor you."

Murmurs of agreement circled the table as Sarah smiled at Chloe.

"That would be wonderful," Sarah said, "thank you. But on one condition."

"Name it," Chloe said.

"We have to be coauthors," Sarah said. "And you get top billing."

"OK," Chloe said, "but I get to choose the font size for the names."

"Oh, I see," Sarah said, squinting at Chloe. "So you can make my name bigger than yours?"

"That's some solid negotiating, right there," Dennis said as the table laughed.

"I suppose I have no choice but to agree," Sarah said with a smile. She shared a look with Antoine, who gave her a nod. "But wait a moment: I have a question. Going back to the all-access web courses and the big livestream—we may have a problem there. How are you going to pull it off without a COO?"

"What do you mean?" Dennis said, looking confused.

"I knew you two were up to something," Linda said. "Come on, out with it."

Antoine laughed, a deep, rich sound. "Well, I've decided to retire."

"What?" Linda blurted, sharing a shocked look with Dennis.

Antoine held up his hands. "It's time. I'm pushing seventy-five now, and the wife and I want to get some traveling in. I talked it over with Sarah, and she gave her blessing. But don't worry—we've already found a replacement."

"Who?" Dennis said.

Antoine settled his gaze on Joyce. She looked back, a puzzled smile on her face. After glancing at Sarah, her smile faded and her eyes grew wide. "Me?"

Linda smacked the table. "Of course. Joyce is the perfect choice!"

Joyce began shaking her head. "No, I—"

"Yes, it has to be!" Dennis agreed.

"All those in favor?" Sarah intoned, smiling.

"Aye!" Antoine, Dennis, and Linda shouted in unison.

"Chloe?" Joyce said.

Chloe smiled, more than a little relieved at the development. "Aye," she laughed. "Definitely, aye."

"And what about you, Joyce?" Sarah asked.

"I—I don't know," Joyce said. "Wouldn't Dennis or Linda be better?"

"Joyce, dear," Linda said, "you damn near run the show already. Ever since Sarah brought you on, we haven't had to lift a finger for her. You've been more than an assistant from the start."

"It makes sense, doesn't it?" Sarah said. "The COO helps the CEO with whatever duties are needed. You've been doing that for years, making things a lot easier for Antoine along the way. And since Chloe is going to be the new CEO, it makes even more sense. You two have been joined at the hip since she got here. So what do you say?"

A tear streamed down Joyce's face as she nodded. "OK. Yes. Thank you so much."

"You have to say 'aye' or it isn't official," Dennis teased.

Joyce's breath hitched as she laughed. "Aye."

"The ayes have it," Sarah said. "The motion carries."

A round of cheers went up as Chloe and Joyce shared an excited look, both with tears in their eyes.

"And now, Joyce," Sarah continued, "for your first act as COO, would you kindly see to that special bottle we set aside?"

"Oh, of course," Joyce said, wiping her eyes and darting from the room.

"What's this about, now?" Dennis asked.

"Just a little something I'd like to do while my nurse is out of earshot," Sarah said.

Joyce returned with a bottle of champagne and a serving tray of glasses, setting both on the table. "Who would like to do the honors?" she asked, holding up the bottle.

"Speaking from many years of experience," Antoine said, "that is strictly COO business."

"He's right," Dennis said. "It's in every charter across the land."

"OK," Joyce said as she fiddled with the foil.

"Whoa, is that Dom Perignon?" Frank asked.

"It is," Sarah confirmed. "Important occasions like this one call for the best." She glanced over her shoulder. "And if Betty comes in, you guys gave me sparkling grape juice, got it?"

The group agreed, laughing and talking as Joyce popped the cork and filled the glasses, distributing them around the table before resuming her seat.

After setting Duke on the floor, Sarah moved to stand. Chloe and Joyce made to help her, but she held up a hand, warding them off. With some effort, she stood and raised her glass aloft as the table fell silent. "Some of you I've known for many years. Some, not nearly as long as I would have liked. But one and all, it has been my great pleasure to know you—to work with you, to laugh with you, to dream with you. And it is my sole wish that you continue working, laughing, and dreaming together, so that those who come after you may better do the same. To each of you, to all of us, and to all those yet to come. Cheers."

"Cheers," the group echoed.

CHAPTER NINE

The Horses

The next few days were difficult. Sarah's condition grew considerably worse, prompting Betty to call the doctor. He adjusted her meds, sharing that she soon wouldn't be able to leave her bed. After the celebration just a few nights prior, Chloe found the quiet and stillness that fell over the house alarming—though not nearly as alarming as its suddenness.

While trying and failing to get some work done in her attic apartment one afternoon, Chloe welcomed the sound of Joyce ascending the staircase.

"She's taking a final trip outside," Joyce said. "She'd like you to meet her at the south stable."

"OK," Chloe said. "You're not coming?"

"Nah, this is between you two. She has some news."

"Oh? Good or bad?"

Joyce smiled. "Can't say. That's privileged COO information."

Chloe barked a laugh. "Sworn to secrecy, huh? OK, I see how it is."

Throwing her sneakers on, she made her way down the paved lane toward the barn. Clouds loomed overhead, the kind that cooled the air without threatening rain. In the distance, she saw a number of ranch hands leading horses. They appeared to be headed for the same destination. Although she had been there for nearly a month, she realized that she had yet to visit any of the barns. She assumed she'd get her chance when she took Lewis up on his offer for riding lessons, but she'd been so busy with work, she had yet to follow through.

Though they called it a stable, to Chloe it appeared more like a barn. Two stories high, with large double doors at each end, it also had a set of glass double doors on the lengthwise side facing the lane, under a small triangular roof. Inside, a large glass display stood against the wall opposite the door, stretching some ten yards wide. Chloe's jaw dropped as she realized it was dedicated to Sarah—dozens upon dozens of dressage trophies, ribbons, and plaques, many with photos of her standing next to various horses. Some even showed Bob Proctor standing next to her. Some photos dated back decades, while others were as recent as a few years ago. Nearly all the recent ones showed the same horse—a black thoroughbred named Shadow.

Lewis appeared through a door a short way down the hall. Whip-thin, with a salt-and-pepper beard and a deep tan, he looked as if he'd been born in his old jeans, scuffed cowboy boots, and tattered short-sleeved flannel shirt. He had an easy way about him, though Chloe couldn't say why. She didn't know him very well, but he felt like someone she could talk to.

"Pretty impressive, huh?" he said, glancing over the trophies.

Chloe nodded. "I'll say. I had no idea."

"Not many do. You should see the rest."

"What? There's more?"

Lewis laughed, walking back the way he came. "You ready? She's waitin' on us."

"Sure, yeah," Chloe said, breaking her eyes away from the case and rushing to catch up.

The two took a few turns down a hall, soon arriving at a wide brick aisle that ran the length of the building to the large barn doors at each end, both opened wide. Each side of the aisle housed a row of stables, many of which were occupied. An air of activity surrounded the place as several ranch hands went about various duties. She followed Lewis to the western end of the barn. Just outside the doors, parked in the grass near the edge of the paved path, sat Sarah in her wheelchair, with Betty standing nearby.

"Thanks, Betty," Sarah said. "Chloe will bring me back in a bit."

Chloe and Betty waved to each other as the nurse turned back to the house.

Approaching Sarah, Chloe bent down and gave her a hug. "How are you feeling?"

"Oh, pretty good," Sarah replied. "The weather's cooler. It felt like a good day to say goodbye to the horses. I wanted to share it with you."

"I'd like that," Chloe said.

"Ready, ma'am?" Lewis called from the barn.

"Ready," Sarah replied.

Just inside the doors, a hand passed the lead of a horse to Lewis. A brown mare with a braided mane, she clopped along beside him, nickering when she noticed Sarah.

"Oh, this is Clover," Sarah said, holding out her hands as the horse dropped her head low. Sniffing Sarah's hair, Clover nudged her muzzle against Sarah's shoulder. "She was foaled by Jasmine, what, ten years ago, Lewis?"

"Nearabouts," Lewis said.

Sarah caressed Clover's jaw. "Feel, Chloe."

Chloe reached out a hand, and Clover nuzzled it. She patted the horse's neck, feeling the muscles ripple beneath its thick coat. "Wow."

"Incredible, aren't they?" Sarah said.

"Yeah," Chloe agreed. "It's been so long. I forgot how big and powerful they are."

"That's what I love about them," Sarah said. Clover nickered again, and Sarah laughed. "She smells the apples. Can you grab me one?"

"Sure," Chloe said. A canvas bag hung heavy from the handle of the wheelchair. Reaching in, she pulled one out and handed it to Sarah.

"It's their physicality, sure," Sarah continued, cutting the apple in half with a pocketknife as Clover nudged her arm. "But it's their nature as well that amazes me. So powerful, yet so calm." She held half the apple in her palm. Clover took it gently, nodding her head as she chewed. "They feel every bit as much as we do, and in the center of that feeling is a peace we humans rarely know. They understand life in a way few of us can. No thoughts of tomorrow, no worries over yesterday. They are *here*, in every sense of the word. You can feel that presence when you see them, when you touch them." She fed Clover the other half and caressed her neck. "When you ride them, when you get the feel of each other and move as one, you can get a small glimpse at the world through their eyes. And it's a far more beautiful place than we can ever imagine."

Sarah nodded to Lewis. He turned Clover around and headed back to the barn, passing the lead off to one ranch hand. Another stood waiting with the next horse.

Sarah let out a soft gasp. "That's Major. A chestnut thoroughbred. He was trained for competitive dressage until we retired him several years ago. I won one of my last medals with him. A national event in Louisville. Remarkably good with kids. He's one of our best training horses now."

At least a few hands taller than Clover, Major bent his head low to Sarah's waiting arms. Ears forward, he kept nudging her gently, as if he knew something was wrong. Chloe ran a hand over his neck, feeling the soft strands of his mane.

"What do you feel when you touch them?" Sarah asked. "When you look in their eyes?"

Chloe shook her head. "I don't know. Awe, mostly. And this weird sense that—I don't know. Like they're equipped with something we're not."

"Exactly," Sarah said, gesturing toward the bag. Chloe retrieved an apple as she continued. "Like a perception we don't have access to. Like they come from a place no other living creature originates. A more profound place, one that imbues them with a wisdom that's beyond us. It gives them an awareness just a few degrees removed from the rest of us, allowing them to know things we can only guess at. Allowing them to understand life in ways we simply can't."

Chloe nodded as she stroked his mane. "It's like they are creatures that don't believe in farewells."

"Yes," Sarah said, feeding him the two halves of the apple, first one and then the other. "And since we are creatures who must say farewells, I would have them be happy ones."

She nodded to Lewis, and he turned Major back to the barn.

"While we have a moment, Chloe, you should know something."

Chloe knelt beside her, resting an elbow on the arm of her wheelchair. "What's that?"

Sarah smiled at her, brushing a strand of hair out of Chloe's eyes. She took Chloe's hand in hers. "I had my attorney stop by this week. We concluded the paperwork on a few final matters. I wanted you to be here today because while I'm saying goodbye to the horses, you're saying hello."

"What do you mean?"

"They belong to you now."

Chloe stared at Sarah, shocked. "What? Sarah, that's—"

"The best thing for the horses, I know," Sarah interjected. "And for you."

Sarah began laughing, and Chloe realized her mouth was hanging open. She couldn't think of anything to say.

"But you'll need a place to house the horses," Sarah continued, "which is why I'm giving you the barns. And the land they're on. And the house. The entire ranch, in fact."

Chloe didn't know when she'd started crying, but she was.

"Lastly," Sarah said, "I have a controlling interest in the institute. So you don't just run it now. You own it."

"No," Chloe said weakly. "You can't."

"Come here," Sarah said, opening her arms.

Chloe moved to the front of the wheelchair and wrapped her arms around Sarah's waist, burying her head in her shoulder. Sarah cradled her, smoothing her hair while she kissed the top of her head. Chloe didn't know why, but that just made her cry all the harder—as if she were only just realizing that she was going to lose her best friend.

"You'll be OK," Sarah whispered, rocking her back and forth. "You'll be more than OK. You'll be great. You're going to do great things."

After a few more minutes of Sarah's soothing, she was finally able to regain her composure. Pulling away, Chloe looked up at her. "It's too much." She didn't know if she was talking about the inheritance or the thought of going on without Sarah.

"Only for a time," Sarah said. "Just remember this. Everything you need to know"—she nodded toward the barn and the horses—"you can learn from them."

"I'll remember," Chloe said, climbing to her feet. A little embarrassed, she was glad to see that Lewis had waited at the barn. Dusting herself off, she wiped her eyes and returned to her spot next to the wheelchair.

With a wave from Sarah, Lewis returned with a third horse. Then a fourth. And a fifth. Sarah said goodbye to over two dozen horses that afternoon, while Chloe said hello. The last in line was the one that appeared in so many of the trophy case's photos.

"This is Shadow," Sarah told her. Now gray at the muzzle and forehead, the once pure-black horse appeared leaner than the rest, with a small dip in her back and a stiff stride. Yet her eyes were still clear, and upon seeing Sarah, her head perked up and her steps quickened. For a moment, Chloe could see the tall, regal champion from the photos. Shadow placed her muzzle at Sarah's cheek, refusing to move even when offered an apple. Nickering from time to time, she closed her eyes as Sarah stroked her faced and whispered to her. Chloe pretended not to notice when Lewis turned away, wiping his cheek with a hand.

After several minutes, Sarah was able to pry Shadow's muzzle away and feed her the two apple halves. Sitting in silence, the horse chomped away, her eyes never straying far from Sarah. Giving Shadow a final pat, Sarah nodded toward Lewis, but it became clear that Shadow had no intention of leaving. She wouldn't budge from her spot next to the wheelchair.

Laughing, with tears in her eyes, Sarah looked up at Chloe. "Let's head back to the house. She'll follow him once I'm farther away. And toss Lewis another apple. That should help."

Taking up position behind the wheelchair, Chloe threw Lewis an apple and turned onto the paved path. But Shadow's insistent nickering turned them around. She was yanking at the lead, all but dragging Lewis up the path toward them.

"Almost as stubborn as you," Lewis called to Sarah.

"Almost," Sarah said, laughing again. "All right, girl, all right. Let's go back together. Maybe she'll calm down once I'm inside."

Lewis let go of the lead, and Shadow kept pace beside the wheelchair all the way to the house, her head low, where Sarah could reach it. Once at the porch, she gave Shadow a hug, stretching her arms as far around the horse's head as she could reach.

With a final pat on the neck, Sarah turned to Lewis. "Is there a strapping young cowboy who can carry me up the porch?"

"I dunno about strapping or young, but I got the cowboy part down pat," Lewis said. Cradling Sarah in his arms, he carried her up the steps as Chloe wrestled the wheelchair up behind them. Once Sarah was settled back in place, Lewis took Shadow's lead, the extra apple at the ready.

"Goodbye, love," Sarah said, blowing Shadow a kiss. She patted Chloe's hand where it rested on her shoulder, and Chloe turned the wheelchair toward the house.

Glancing out a window several minutes later, Chloe saw that Lewis had only just begun to coax Shadow back to the barn.

CHAPTER TEN

FAREWELLS AND NEW DAYS

Finishing her run the following morning, Chloe topped a rise near the house and came upon a strange sight—a horse in the backyard. Horses at the ranch were a common sight, but always with a rider or someone tending to them, and never so close to the house. Closing the distance, she realized it wasn't just any horse. It was Shadow. She had a feeling the old girl was a bit of a troublemaker. She must have gotten out somehow during the night.

Chloe slowed to a walk, then a stop. Something wasn't right. A pang of dread slid through her heart like a knife—Shadow was standing outside Sarah's window. Chloe stood there, wondering if she was just letting her imagination run away with her. Sprinting for the porch, she took the steps two at a time and crashed through the front door. Rushing down the hall and to the back of the house, she found Betty hovered over Sarah where she lay in her bed. Meeting Chloe's eyes, the nurse shook her head.

After a few moments, Betty moved toward the door. "I'm so sorry, Chloe. I'll go make the necessary calls."

Chloe wasn't sure if she'd said anything in response. She may have nodded. Moving to the old side-hung windows near the bed, she flipped the latch and swung them wide. Shadow approached, nickering softly as she stuck her head inside. Falling silent, she nudged the side of the bed with her muzzle.

Chloe stroked the horse's neck. "Hello, Shadow." She repeated the greeting, over and over, as the two said goodbye to their friend.

*   *   *

Several months later, on a warm spring afternoon at the Meadowood resort in the Napa Valley, Chloe looked out over the south lawn at the audience of over four hundred people. Heaving a sigh to help calm her nerves, she focused her thoughts on everything it had taken to reach this moment.

After the funeral service, condolences had poured in from all over the world. The audience for the livestream event commemorating Sarah's life and achievements numbered in the tens of thousands. Then Chloe soldiered through a whirlwind of meetings with attorneys, the leadership team, the media, and more. After several weeks, she'd finally been able to take a breath and get back to writing. Looking back, she didn't know how she would have done it without Joyce.

Chloe spent the next several months helping the team grow the publishing and youth divisions while writing Sarah's final book and picking away on her novel series. Frank and Claire took to the work like ducks to water, and within just a few months, Frank took the plunge and left the Gate to work for the institute full-time. At Chloe's insistence, the couple did finally spend some time at the Meadowood—a full week of fun and relaxation, courtesy of Chloe and the rest of the team. Claire loved every moment, and Frank nearly had a good time.

When they returned from their vacation, they helped Chloe refine her coauthored book. In keeping with Sarah's wishes, they had the cover designer give Chloe top billing—though with a smaller font than Sarah's. With the book finalized, they began planning publication and a speaking tour—but first, Chloe had to promote her debut fiction novel, *Sunset at Whisper Creek*. It became an instant best seller, with critics and audiences clamoring for the next installment in the series, slated for the following year.

As Chloe looked over the crowd at Meadowood, she was glad she had the experience of that book tour under her belt. Holding interviews and readings gave her the chance to sharpen her speaking skills, and she was going to need them today. The event represented a celebration of several milestones rolled into one—Sarah's final book, Chloe's first book written for the institute, and the first book published by the institute's new publication division—which, after a vote from the leadership team, came to be called Proctor Garner Daniels Press. They thought it appropriate to have Chloe's last name risen to the same heights as the institute's founders—an honor she promised she'd spend her life living up to.

Chloe had reserved the front row for special guests, and she was glad to see that they were all able to attend. She remembered Kendra from her group way back at that first conference at the Hilton in L.A., where Chloe was first introduced to Sarah. When she started Sarah's program, Kendra was barely making a living doing two part-time jobs. Now, having grown her small business exponentially, the bubbly entrepreneur was the proud face of an entire lifestyle brand sweeping the country. Today Kendra was decked out in her latest spring attire, including her trademark decorative scarf. She made little claps with her hands while talking excitedly with the woman behind her.

To Kendra's right sat Jason, the big security guard who, on a whim, had given Sarah's Unstuck program a chance. Joyce had informed Chloe that he now owned a small fleet of food trucks in L.A., a lifelong dream of his. Rumor had it that he and Kendra had become an item (as Sarah had suspected from the start). Chloe smiled as Kendra absently reached for his hand while talking with her neighbor, proving the rumor true.

Michelle sat to Jason's right. The marketing agency owner had expanded as well. Her agency now served clients all over the world, with three offices and counting throughout the country.

Further down the front row sat a group nearly as rambunctious as Kendra—Andre and Talia, with their teenage twins. Joyce had informed her that the family had grown much closer since implementing the program, which the couple was sure had a hand in elevating their son and daughter to valedictorian and salutatorian of their class.

The rest of the front row featured the Meadowood team. Featuring some of the most successful people in the world, Chloe was flattered that they'd taken time out of their busy schedules to attend. Ricardo Costa of the Ding! social media platform conversed with Lisa Beaumont, the founder of Gaia Electric. Since they had implemented the program at their companies, both productivity and employee morale were at all-time highs.

Next to them sat Min, the STEM researcher, who was chatting with Sidney and Tom, the software engineer couple experimenting with augmented reality and virtual reality. Both parties had reported to Joyce that their research was progressing in leaps and bounds since starting the program—and with a little help from Ricardo and Lisa, they had received a great deal of attention from some highly interested investors. As the din of the excited crowd filled the green expanse of the south lawn, Chloe was almost overwhelmed with gratitude. They had all come so far, in such a short amount of time.

A tap on her shoulder brought her out of the moment.

"It's time," Joyce said.

"OK," Chloe replied with a nervous smile, giving her a hug.

Joyce hugged her back, then pulled away to adjust Chloe's collar and check her hair. "You got this."

Stepping from behind a small partition and up onto the stage, Chloe made her way to the podium as the audience erupted in applause. The front row stood, cheering her on, and like an ocean wave, the rest of the crowd followed.

"Thank you," Chloe laughed as she adjusted the microphone. "Thank you very much. Wow." After what felt like an embarrassingly long time, they finally settled back into their seats. Looking at the crowd from this new vantage, Chloe let the gratitude she felt wash over her.

"I am here because of another. As are you. But before I talk about her, I have a question for you." She paused, giving the audience a smile.

"What do you know about monarch butter-flies?"